Original title:
Leaves and Limericks

Copyright © 2025 Creative Arts Management OÜ
All rights reserved.

Author: Helena Marchant
ISBN HARDBACK: 978-1-80567-296-8
ISBN PAPERBACK: 978-1-80567-595-2

Mischief Among Sturdy Branches

In a tree where squirrels gnaw,
A raccoon sneaks as quiet as straw.
He steals a bright snack,
Turns tail with a clack.

The owl hoots, 'Now isn't that raw!'
As a woodpecker taps on the bark.
A party unfolds,
With giggles untold,
And shadows dance light in the dark.

A branch sways low, what a sight,
A chubby chipmunk takes flight.
He leaps with a cheer,
No hint of a fear,
An acorn dashed down in delight.

The tree creaks, with mischief amassed,
As giggling friends swirl by fast.
With whispers abound,
Joy's fully found,
In this merry wood, unsurpassed.

Cadence of Colorful Echoes

Bright hues twirl through the breeze,
With a flutter that aims to please.
A butterfly prances,
In winged romances,
And dances with gusto and ease.

The sun peeks through soft verdant can,
As dandelions take their grand stand.
A patch of sweet blooms,
Breaks winter's dull dooms,
And paints the green land like a band.

With chatter from branches we hear,
A parrot that won't disappear.
He squawks a mad rhyme,
In melodious time,
As giggles break through the clear.

From twig to the tip of the branch,
The critters all wiggle and dance.
What joy to behold,
Their antics unfold,
While nature throws down a grand chance.

Tales from a Tangled Treetop

Up high where the whispers are true,
A curious cat takes a view.
With eyes all aglow,
She watches the show,
As the world wears a leafy debut.

A lemur swings by with a grin,
While the bluebirds all chirp and spin.
They rally for fun,
In the warm golden sun,
As the mischief begins to imbue.

A brisk breeze shakes loose a small nut,
It lands with a thud, what a cut!
The squirrel screams loud,
In a giggling crowd,
As they watch the old branch give a tut.

Each moment a tale in the air,
With laughter that's light as a prayer.
Under this green dome,
Friends find their home,
In a world that delights everywhere.

Syllables of Sunlit Canopies

Sunlight spills joy on the ground,
As critters and giggles surround.
A playful young ram,
Spins round like a clam,
In melodies soft and profound.

The shadows then stretch and they tease,
As a breeze whispers tales through the trees.
A frog gives a croak,
With a giggling joke,
While the ants march in perfect degrees.

Quick twitch of a tail draws a cheer,
From all of the friends gathered near.
With hops and with skips,
No worry—just quips,
As laughter rings out in the sphere.

From boughs to the green, there's a glee,
Where whispers flow light as a bee.
In bright canopy sway,
They dance through the day,
In a frolicsome world, wild and free.

Mischievous Melodies in the Meadow

In the meadow, a frog played a tune,
With a wiggle and hop under the moon.
He croaked out a rhyme,
In rhythm and time,
Chasing crickets that danced like a cartoon.

A squirrel with a hat joined the spree,
Juggling acorns with glee, oh so free.
With a twirl and a twist,
He couldn't resist,
Tumbling down from the highest oak tree.

Harmonies of Humming Breezes

A bumblebee buzzed with a grin,
Tickling daisies from within.
He hummed all day,
In a silly way,
As the flowers around him spun and swirled in.

The wind played a joke with a gust,
On the butterflies, sending them just
To flutter and sway,
In a comical play,
Riding high on a joke, full of trust.

A Comedy of Organic Dances

A rabbit in socks took the stage,
With a leap and a flip, such a rage.
The audience cheered,
As he loudly steered,
Through a dance that would surely enrage.

A turtle in shades came next,
Moving slow, causing all to feel vexed.
His groove was a treat,
With rhythm so neat,
In the slowest of steps, he perplexed.

Ballads of Bright Burgeoning

A sunflower sang with bright flair,
Challenging daisies to dare.
With a voice that could boom,
In full floral bloom,
It declared a bright concert, so rare.

A hedgehog with maracas kept beat,
Shaking them fast with joy and with heat.
As the tune filled the air,
Every critter laid bare,
Joined in laughter and fun on their feet.

Vibrant Whispers of Nature's Blessing

In the breeze, a joke takes flight,
A tumble and twist, oh what a sight!
An acorn did laugh, what a tease,
As squirrels dance madly with ease.

The sun plays tag with shadows long,
Flowers nodding, humming a song.
Petals twirl in a silly spree,
Nature's jesters, wild and free.

Chronicles in the Shady Nook

In the nook where giggles grow,
A dragonfly puts on a show.
It zips and dips with flair so grand,
While crickets snap to a beat so planned.

Mushrooms wear hats in colors bright,
As ants march on, what a curious sight!
The owls chuckle, perched so high,
With one eye closed, the other wry.

The Jest of the Changing Seasons

The frost comes in with sneaky toes,
While pumpkins grin beneath their glows.
A snowman winks, all dressed in white,
Sipping cider, oh what delight!

Then spring pops up with a joyful shout,
As tulips bloom and the bees buzz about.
Chasing rainbows with a hop and skip,
While clouds share jokes on a sunbeam trip.

A Medley of Dappled Hue

Colors dance in a playful spree,
Orange and gold, wild and free.
A brown squirrel with a cheeky grin,
Steals a berry, oh what a win!

A rustling sound, a chuckle near,
As the wind whispers, "Come over here!"
With giggles shared among the trees,
Nature's antics, sure to please.

Tangles of a Treetop Tale

In a tree there danced a squirrel,
Wearing nuts like a great big pearl.
He took a silly leap,
And made the whole crowd weep,
As he twirled in a spin and swirl.

A crow cawed loud, what a show!
The chipmunks laughed, oh how they glow.
With acorns on their heads,
And wild, silly threads,
They tumbled down in the row.

Dances of the Shifting Shade

Underneath the swaying boughs,
A troupe of ants take their vows.
With tiny few steps,
And humorous reps,
They moonwalk like royalty now.

A shadow zipped, quite a fright,
A rabbit bounced in pure delight.
With carrots he pranced,
In an odd little dance,
As daylight turned to the night.

A Symphony of Petals and Puns

A butterfly sang with a flair,
As the daisies all fluffed their hair.
With jests in the breeze,
They giggled with ease,
While petals fell down everywhere.

A honeybee buzzed with a grin,
Spreading laughter as it did spin.
Then pollen took flight,
In a most silly sight,
As flowers all welcomed their kin.

The Witty Wind's Serenade

There once was a wind full of glee,
That played with the branches of trees.
It whispered and swayed,
In a jocular parade,
Sending giggles through every spree.

With a whoosh and a jump, oh so spry,
The clouds in the sky seemed to fly.
They donned silly hats,
And danced with the cats,
As they twirled in the bright blue sky.

Odes to Whispering Canopies

Beneath the trees, secrets unfold,
Squirrels are plotting, or so I've been told.
A leaf fell right down,
It landed on Brown,
His hat's now a crown, shining with gold.

The branches get tickled by breezes so light,
Each rustle invites a grand playful fight.
A gust made a dance,
That made all hearts prance,
Even the shadows, in laughter, take flight.

Jests of the Changeful Season

The sun wears a hat that's starting to fade,
While clouds in their pajamas come out to parade.
A flurry of fluff
Makes jaunts rather tough,
But laughter's the warm drink that's freshly made.

With sweaters and shorts, the townsfolk all meet,
They skip through the puddles, avoiding defeat.
One slip and a splash,
A sudden, bright crash,
Now the lamppost's got soggy, wet feet!

Spirals of Fluttering Colors

A whirl of ochre, a wink of bright red,
The ground wears a quilt where all prancers tread.
A tumble, a twirl,
A gust makes it swirl,
Like nature's own jest with ribbons spread.

The artist claims colors can't pop quite like this,
But faced with a gust, they twirl up in bliss.
They spin through the air,
Without a single care,
And leave us all wondering which way is a miss.

Eccentric Echoes in the Grove

In the grove where the giggles of branches unite,
The critters hold court, sharing tales of their fright.
A frog with a grin,
Said, "Jump in, have a spin!"
While crickets sing songs that shiver with delight.

A mole made a joke about tunnels so deep,
While owls sat like lords, plotting what they could reap.
A chuckle from high,
As one bird flew by,
Announced, "Life's a stroll, and the world's ours to keep!"

Captivating Stories in the Currents

In a whispering brook, fish dance with glee,
Telling fishy tales of a faraway sea.
A turtle in shades of bright yellow glow,
Claims he's the fastest, oh what a show!

A frog hops along with a crown on his head,
Singing out loud as he's hopping instead.
Telling the world that he's royal and grand,
While tripping on flies that get stuck in the sand.

The Humor of Fading Shades

In twilight's soft glow, a squirrel took flight,
Chasing shadows that danced in the light.
He tripped on a twig, fell down with a thud,
Where laughter erupted from the nearby mud.

A wise old owl perched in a tree,
Hooted so loud, 'You're all just like me!'
His feathers resplendent, a grad of the night,
Told the best jokes 'til dawn's early light.

Pranks of the Prismatic Meadow

In a meadow of colors, a butterfly pranks,
Playing tag with the flowers and smiling with thanks.
A daisy lost its hat, it went flying away,
Making all the bees giggle the whole sunny day!

The ladybug chuckles, 'I'll join in the fun!'
Wearing a dandelion crown, enjoying the sun.
Blowing kisses to petals and taking a spin,
As the meadow erupts in giggles and grins.

Rhyme and Rove of Nature's Jests

In the forest so lush, a fox tells a tale,
Of a cat who once tried to catch a big whale.
The trees sway in laughter, their branches a dance,
While a hedgehog rolls by, blissfully entranced.

A raccoon in a mask steals grapes from the vine,
Declaring, 'I'm a bandit, these grapes are all mine!'
But the grapes roll away with a giggle and cheer,
And the raccoon just laughs as they disappear.

A Tidal Wave of Autumnal Echoes

In the park, something swayed,
A swirling dance, they played.
With a crunch and a flutter,
They'd giggle and mutter.

Squirrels plotted a heist,
For goodies, they were enticed.
But slipped on a nut,
And fell with a gut!

One shouted, "This isn't so nice!"
As laughter rolled like dice.
A dance of delight,
As day turned to night.

Soon they'd gather again,
With mischief they'd pen.
In the chaos, they'd cheer,
For the fun of the year!

The Ballad of Petal Paths

Once I strolled with a grin,
Through a world full of spin.
A flower with flair,
Said, "Stop! Don't you dare!"

It twirled, and then sneezed,
At the wind it appeased.
Then petals flew high,
Like confetti, oh my!

A bumblebee buzzed,
In a dance he was fuzzed.
He tripped on the vine,
And began to define.

With giggles and fun,
The sun started to run.
Petal paths paved in glee,
In this world, wild and free!

Nature's Melodies in Soft Decay

Oh, the whispers of gray,
In the trees that sway.
A tune that is funny,
Like bees that sing honey.

With notes that rebound,
Through the thickets abound.
Chirps of a sparrow,
Swaying to an old marrow.

There's a rustle, a cheer,
As the grubs all draw near.
An earthworm plays bass,
While the rabbits keep pace!

Together they dance,
In a joyous expanse.
Nature's show, oh so grand,
With laughter we stand!

Enchantment of the Rustling Veil

Beneath a canopy bright,
A scene of pure delight.
With rustles and peeps,
The giggles in heaps!

A fox in a cap,
Took a humorous nap.
He dreamed of a stew,
With a side of green goo!

A rabbit gave pause,
To inspect the cause.
He jumped with a bound,
For new friends he found!

In the shimmer of light,
Their antics took flight.
An enchanting ballet,
In the woodlands at play!

A Waltz of Warm Tones

In autumn's gown, a dance so bright,
The branches sway in pure delight.
A squirrel prances, tail held high,
While acorns drop like pie from pie.

With every twirl, a joke takes flight,
The forest chuckles in the light.
A chipmunk sings a silly tune,
Dancing 'neath the silly moon.

The Frolic of the Wealthy Wilderness

In fields where fortunes laugh and play,
A bear in shades of rich array.
With berry hats and nuts in hand,
He juggles snacks like they were planned.

The wealthy 'coon with pockets wide,
Struts in the sun with too much pride.
He trips on roots, then laughs away,
His grand display—oh, what a day!

A Tapestry of Turbulent Tints

In colors bright, a chaos swirls,
A flamingo wraps in colors' twirls.
With paint-splashed wings, it lands with grace,
And makes the flowers laugh in place.

A parrot yells a cheeky jest,
While dragonflies prepare a fest.
They buzz around, a buzzing choir,
Making the vivid hues transpire.

Rhyme Among the Glorious Green

In emerald realms where giggles roam,
The frogs make croaks their happy home.
With every leap, they crack a joke,
A playful spin brings laughter's cloak.

The daisies sway, and tease the breeze,
While bunnies hop with hops of ease.
A rhyme is found in every nook,
As nature serves a jolly book.

Whispers of Autumn's Caress

In a park where the squirrels vie,
A jester hat flies through the sky.
With a pirouette bold,
And a tale to be told.

The trees chuckle softly with glee,
As the wind sings a tune wild and free.
One leaf took a leap,
And the laughter won't sleep.

Each gust brings a giggling spree,
While the critters dance freely with glee.
Beneath branches so wide,
They jest and they glide.

With a tickle of air in the trees,
And a hint of mischief that teases.
Life's a grand jest,
In this autumnal quest.

The Dance of Falling Fables

A storyteller sways in the breeze,
With old yarns that aim to please.
Each twist, each turn,
Makes the wild critters yearn.

A rabbit with glasses notes down,
The antics of all in the town.
From the shy to the bold,
Every tale, pure gold.

Dancing shadows, they hop and they play,
With the stories that brighten the day.
In the twilight's embrace,
Feels like teasing a face.

With chuckles that sprinkle the night,
And the moon playing tag with the light.
Such whimsical fun,
Round each corner they run.

Stanzas Under the Canopy

In a forest where giggles reform,
Where the branches are twisted and warm.
The owls play charades,
While the raccoons invade.

A fox dressed in feathers appears,
And he juggles while sipping his peers.
With each woop and woof,
The trees raise a roof.

The bonds of this merry old clan,
Are a blend of the lively and plan.
Each rustle a rhyme,
Dancing all through time.

With no worries, just fun on the mend,
Where the stories wrap round every bend.
It's a laughter parade,
In the twilight cascade.

Green Verses in the Wind

A shepherd of stories stands high,
With a grin that could catch the sly cry.
He fluffs up his tail,
And sets off on a trail.

With the wind as his trusty old friend,
Together, their giggles won't end.
Spinning tales in the air,
Of mischief and flair.

A dance on the tips of the grass,
While the shadows and moonlight all pass.
The banter flies free,
As they sip wild tea.

In a world that's a whimsical spree,
With each twist, they invent a new key.
Their giggles ring loud,
In the night's fancied shroud.

The Humorous Heart of the Forest

A squirrel with a hat danced a jig,
He thought he was grand, not a twig.
But slipped on a nut,
And fell with a thud,
In front of a crow who called, "You big!"

The rabbit wore shoes made of cheese,
He pranced through the grass with such ease.
But was chased by a cat,
Who found it quite fat,
And said, "Please don't step on my peas!"

A fox recited a poem with flair,
While hedgehogs held hands in the air.
But a gust took the page,
And flew it with rage,
Leaving all of them gasping in despair!

In the heart of the woods, life's a laugh,
Where shadows and giggles do staff.
With folly and fun,
The day's never done,
Each critter a whimsical calf!

Revelry Among Rustling Embers

A raccoon with a crown held a feast,
He invited each friend, to say the least.
But pies made of glue,
Got stuck on a shoe,
So they dined on a marshmallow beast!

The owl gave a speech, all so wise,
But tripped on a root, to surprise!
He flapped in dismay,
As they laughed all the way,
And told him to rethink his next prize!

The fireflies danced in a whirl,
While a dragonfly spun like a girl.
But all of their light,
Flew away in the night,
Leaving them with a wish and a twirl!

In shadows that flicker and glow,
The woodland brings joy from below.
With giggles and cheer,
They banished all fear,
In this revelry's radiant show!

Rhapsody in Verdant Hues

A dandelion sang a sweet tune,
While critters had fun, gone to noon.
But a breeze took a puff,
That wafted quite rough,
Sending all of them flying, oh, swoon!

The turtle played cards with a hare,
Who cheated outright, but didn't care.
To the drum of the beat,
They hopped to their feet,
And danced in the air without a spare!

The hedgehogs broke out in a cheer,
With goggles and capes, what a sphere!
They rolled with such glee,
As they shouted, "Whoopee!"
While the badger just grumbled, "Oh dear!"

In the meadow so bright and so bold,
Where tales of delight are retold.
With laughter they play,
In a whimsical way,
Creating a story of gold!

Giggles Underneath the Woodland

A chipmunk on stilts took a stroll,
He twirled and he laughed with a roll.
But a twig snapped with glee,
And down came the bee,
Who buzzed 'round his head, not so whole!

A field mouse with socks up to here,
Told jokes about cheese and a steer.
But a wink from a gnat,
Brought laughter, all that,
As they spilled all their snacks and some beer!

A wise toad hopped up with some jokes,
Drawing giggles from all of the folks.
Yet the punchline was lost,
And it came at a cost,
When he slipped on the muck—oh, what croaks!

Beneath leafy shades rich in mirth,
The creatures all join for their worth.
With chuckles and fun,
The day's just begun,
Celebrating this whimsical birth!

Petals' Prose in Twilight's Embrace

In twilight's glow, they dance and twirl,
With silly hats, they laugh and swirl.
A pebble hops, a twig slips by,
They chuckle loud, beneath the sky.

One twinkling star, a toss of cream,
A leaf wore shades, like in a dream.
They shared some jokes, both loud and proud,
As shadows stretched, they sang aloud.

The night's balloon burst with a pop,
A witty leaf did a funny flop.
The breeze giggled, the moonlight shone,
As whispers flew from leaf to stone.

A sprite would wink, a rabbit tease,
While singing sweetly in the trees.
In twilight's glow, the fun won't cease,
For nature's jest brings laughter's peace.

The Narrative of Woodland Whispers.

In the glen where critters play,
A squirrel jived, brightening the day.
With tales of acorns, big and round,
He tickled roots beneath the ground.

The badger rolled, in laughter he'd swell,
With stories spun from woodland dwell.
The toad croaked puns, oh what a sight,
While fireflies blinked through the night.

A fox played tricks, a prankster sly,
He left a feather where it shouldn't lie.
The owl just hooted, wise and grand,
His jokes fell flat, like grains of sand.

Yet every giggle filled the air,
With echoes of joy, beyond compare.
In whispers soft, the woods conspire,
To spread the warmth, like a bonfire.

Whispers of Autumn's Canvas

In colors bright, the canvas sways,
With crickets chirping, in playful ways.
The pumpkin chuckled, round and bright,
As ghosts in sheets gave quite a fright.

A scarecrow danced, with arms all wide,
"It's harvest time!" he claimed with pride.
The apples grinned, red and crisp,
While cider waved, a frothy lisp.

The winds did giggle, a playful breeze,
As pumpkins plotted, "Let's scare the bees!"
A crow cawed jokes, perched up so high,
With every cackle that soared the sky.

The night would fall, with stars on stage,
As crickets chirped, and turned the page.
In autumn's air, where laughter thrives,
The whispers dance, as memory drives.

Fragments of Falling Foliage

In the park, a whirlwind twirls,
While giggling leaves take joyful swirls.
A maple shouted, "Catch me, quick!"
But a gust swooped in, made the trick!

The ground did laugh with a crunch and crack,
As colors tumbled, never to lack.
Each flutter danced, a parade so grand,
While nuts conspired, plotting their band.

A leaf once slipped on a dewy path,
And giggled loud at its own math.
The acorns donned their tiny hats,
And cheered on nature's funny chats.

As twilight crept, with whispers clear,
The fall's embrace brought joy and cheer.
In falling hues, they all unite,
To share a laugh, in fading light.

The Soft Murmurs of the Season

A squirrel jumped up with a jolt,
And slipped on a nut at the bolt.
He spun round and round,
Then fell to the ground,
Declaring, 'I'm fine, it's my fault!'

The breeze gave a giggle so sweet,
As it swirled through the park on a fleet.
It tickled the toes,
Of friends in a pose,
In a dance only nature can beat.

Heartbeats in the Green Canopy

A rabbit in shorts took a dive,
In pursuit of a carrot alive.
But tripped on a vine,
Fell into a brine,
And surfaced with foam—what a thrive!

The fox donned a hat made of grass,
Declared with a wink, 'I'm a lass!'
With a flick of his tail,
He swore without fail,
He'd dance through the woods with some sass!

Fay's Horizon in Golden Glow

The sun poured its gold on the stream,
Where fairies all danced—a grand scheme.
With a wink and a spin,
They'd swoosh and they'd grin,
'We'll paint the whole world with a dream!'

An owl with a monocle peered,
With wisdom that all had revered.
He hooted a rhyme,
Took his sweet time,
And laughed as the night finally neared.

Fragments of Wandering Whisper

A chicken who dreamed of the skies,
With wings that began to surprise,
Tried flapping so high,
But landed nearby,
Disguised as a clown in a guise.

The gossiping shrubs told a tale,
Of a snail who was swift as a gale.
But the truth, it was slick,
He tripped on a stick,
And danced like a ship in full sail.

Rhyme in the Rustle

In the park, the grasses sway,
A squirrel naps, but dreams of play,
He spins and twirls, with quite a flair,
His acorn hat, a royal wear.

The dandelions giggle loud,
Their yellow crowns, they feel so proud,
A little breeze sends them afloat,
They dance along, like little boats.

A robin sings in merry tune,
While chasing shadows of the moon,
With every hop, he makes a fuss,
As if to say, "Come join the rush!"

So if you hear a rustling sound,
It's nature's jokes that circle 'round,
With every twist, and silly glance,
There's laughter here, come join the dance!

The Palette of a Breezy Day

A canvas stretched, the sky so blue,
With fluffy clouds all painted too,
The sun beams down, a golden brush,
While flowers giggle in the hush.

The tulips bow with colors bright,
Waving petals, pure delight,
A bumblebee hums quite a tune,
As butterflies perform a swoon.

The grass sings softly, tickling toes,
As playful winds begin to pose,
The daisies stretch, they twist and spin,
In this grand art, let joy begin!

So stroll along, embrace the play,
The masterpiece of every day,
With laughter and a splash of cheer,
Nature's humor, oh so near!

Nature's Playful Verses

A cheeky raccoon wears a mask,
Searching for snacks, quite a task,
With nimble paws, he finds a treat,
In a picnic basket, oh, what a feat!

The wind whispers jokes, oh so sly,
As squirrels perform their acrobatics high,
With flips and leaps, they make us grin,
As if they know where the fun begins!

The flowers stretch for the warm sun's ray,
And giggle when the bees dance play,
Each petal, a page from nature's book,
Inviting us all with a joyful look.

So come, dear friend, and join the fun,
In this wild world, we all are one,
Nature's jesters, in green and gold,
With stories of laughter waiting to be told!

The Dance of Green and Gold

Under branches, shadows twirl,
While garden critters laugh and swirl,
The sun dips low, a cheeky grin,
As evening shimmers, let's begin!

With fireflies dressed in glowing hues,
They twinkle bright, like tiny shoes,
A ladybug winks, a marvelous sight,
Inviting all to join her flight.

The trees sway gently, swish and sway,
With nature's band, they start to play,
A tap of roots, a clap of leaves,
A harmony that never leaves.

So dance along with friends so dear,
Embrace the magic, feel no fear,
In this vibrant waltz of green and gold,
Our stories of laughter will unfold!

Puzzles Among the Ponderosas

In the shade of tall trees so bright,
Squirrels dance with pure delight.
They play hide and seek, oh what a thrill,
While trying to catch a rolling pill.

The sun peeks through with a wink,
As hidden treasures rise and sink.
A mystery lies beneath the bark,
With giggles echoing in the park.

Enigmas of the Swaying Oak

An acorn dropped, with such a clatter,
A sleepy owl stirred, what's the matter?
With a flap and a hoot, he flew off course,
Chasing shadows with whimsical force.

The branches creak in disarray,
As critters laugh their cares away.
What secrets dwell in each twist and turn,
While the old oak stands there, wise and stern.

Comedies in the Colorful Canopy

Jays squawk jokes that twist and bend,
As the winds of laughter sweep and send.
A rabbit hops in a witty spree,
Claiming that twigs are fine as can be.

A ladybug winks, dressed in red,
With tiny stripes on her merry head.
She rolls on a leaf, tickled by fate,
Leaving tiny spots for friends to rate.

Serenades of the Shimmering Glade

Fireflies glow with a sparkly cheer,
While ants march on, never a fear.
They sing and dance through the night,
Guided by the moon's soft light.

A raccoon prances in playful delight,
Snatching snacks that are quite a sight.
He juggles nuts with a clumsy grace,
And everyone giggles at his funny face.

The Jingles of Nature's Jests

In a forest where whispers collide,
A squirrel skits with nuts set aside.
It prances and hops,
While laughter just pops,
Making mischief from dusk till the tide.

With a bird on a branch in a hat,
It chirps jokes about a young cat.
The giggles ensue,
As the breeze carries through,
And leaves chuckle, 'Oh, how about that?'

A turtle slips in with a grin,
And the raccoon joins in with a spin.
They dance with delight,
Under twinkling moonlight,
Hosting parties where everyone wins.

Every creature has stories to tell,
Of pranks that went very well.
The laughter erupts,
As each critter jumps up,
In nature's own whimsical shell.

Jest and Jest Again

A fox with a trick up his sleeve,
Played a joke that you wouldn't believe.
With a wink and a nod,
He teased a young prod,
And the laughter would make you reprieve.

A wise old owl perched on high,
Said, "Why not just give it a try?"
With a hoot and a flail,
The stories set sail,
As the tales spread wide in the sky.

A frog in a tux took his place,
He croaked with such elegant grace.
The crowd burst in cheer,
As he tipped quite sincere,
And the laughter rang out in the space.

From hedgehogs to bugs on the ground,
The humor in nature abounds.
In a world full of jest,
It's fun we invest,
For smiles and giggles are found.

Colorful Chronicles of the Wild

The parrot with stories so bold,
Tells of adventures long told.
With feathers so bright,
And a heart full of light,
He makes every tale worth its gold.

A bear in a tutu can dance,
With moves that would make you entrance.
He twirls with delight,
Under stars shining bright,
Inviting all creatures to prance.

A hedgehog in glasses of red,
Claims he knows where all jokes are bred.
With a wink and a smile,
He brings comic style,
For laughter is what he has spread.

In the meadow, the fun never stops,
With rabbits that do silly hops.
They giggle and play,
In a whimsical way,
And joy in their laughter just pops.

The Goblet of Nature's Lore

A magical cup sits on the grass,
It holds all the laughs that can pass.
With a tickle of mirth,
And a burst of sweet girth,
It spills tales of joy unsurpassed.

The badger, the king of the jest,
Claims he only tells jokes at his best.
He juggles some snails,
Recites funny tales,
And the chuckles are hard to contest.

The fireflies flash witty blinks,
As they gather in packs with their kinks.
They twinkle and tease,
As the night passes ease,
Creating a glow that just shrinks.

With a giggle from here to the skies,
Nature's humor just never runs dry.
In a world filled with cheer,
Oh, let's bring them near,
And giggle beneath the night's sigh.

The Amusement of October Whispers

In a park where the breezes dance slow,
A jester in green puts on quite a show.
With a twirl and a spin,
It draws giggles within,
As it tickles the toes of those below.

A gust gives a nudge, off it flies,
Chasing the squirrels under bright skies.
They scamper around,
With laughter resound,
As the trickster comes down with surprise!

Each swirl brings a chuckle or cheer,
It's a time filled with warmth and good beer.
Take a sip and just see,
What fun it can be,
When the rascals come out this time of year!

So gather, my friends, take a seat,
As the chaos dances on nimble feet.
In this autumn delight,
We'll laugh through the night,
For each twirl is a merry repeat.

A Playful Rambunctious Leaf

There once was a leaf with a dream,
To perform in the autumn's grand scheme.
It flopped like a fish,
With each wobbly swish,
Making all of the gardeners beam!

It strutted and pranced with such flair,
The critters would stop and just stare.
With a giggle, it tried,
To spin, flip, and glide,
While the wind played a tune in the air!

But alas, a strong gust had a plan,
To whisk it away as it ran.
With a whoosh and a twirl,
It gave out a whirl,
As it soared like a leaf should—oh man!

Now it's off on a whirlwind spree,
Adventuring wild and free.
It whispers good cheer,
To all those who hear,
A tale full of giggles, you see!

The Chronicle of Color and Chill

In a world painted vibrant and bright,
The chill sneaks in under moonlight.
With each shiver and shake,
The earth starts to quake,
As the hues burst forth in sheer delight.

A chorus of colors begins the show,
As the foliage starts to glow.
With a wink and a grin,
It beckons us in,
To laugh at the changes we know.

The reds, yellows, and oranges unfold,
Tell stories of warmth in the cold.
They giggle and play,
All night and all day,
As they whisper their secrets in bold.

So join in the jubilant spree,
Let's dance with the fizz and the glee.
With each rustling sound,
Joy's waiting around,
To celebrate nature's decree!

The Riddle of Rustling Wonders

What rustles and giggles in glee?
A riddle that beckons like me.
Is it secrets that fly,
Or a joke from the sky,
In the dance of what everyone sees?

A whispering sound, oh so near,
It tickles the senses, bring cheer.
Can you tell what it is,
A mystery fizz,
That makes every October so dear?

With a flick and a flap, it takes flight,
In a caper from morning to night.
Each curve and each sway,
Is a comic ballet,
That leaves us both puzzled and bright!

So the answer, my friend, may just lie,
In the laughter that dances on high.
Each twist of the breeze,
Brings joy with such ease,
In the echoes of autumn's sly cry.

Murmurs of the Painted Trees

In the forest where whispers play,
A squirrel tried to dance one day.
   He slipped on a nut,
   And landed in a rut,
Where clumsy feet had their say.

The oak laughed with glee at his fall,
While the birch waved branches, standing tall.
   The pine held its breath,
   As if that was theft,
Of nature's most graceful brawl.

A rabbit joined in, full of cheer,
With hops that could make others sneer.
   He twirled and he spun,
   In bright autumn's sun,
While the others just rolled in the sphere.

They giggled at tales spun anew,
In colors of red, gold, and blue.
   With twinkles and tricks,
   Nature's own little flicks,
Made time pass like breezes that flew.

Fables in a Spiraling Drift

There once was a hedgehog so sly,
Who fancied that he could fly high.
With wings made from leaves,
He fooled all the neaves,
Until he just fell from the sky.

A parade of old toads croaked aloud,
They jested and gathered a crowd.
"You're not quite a bird,
You've misheard the word,
Now hop in your pond, feeling proud!"

With laughter, they bounced 'round the glen,
The hedgehog hopped back home again.
He learned at the end,
That it's better to bend,
Than to soar like the wind with a pen.

In a world spun with giggles and cheer,
We find hopscotch lies hidden, my dear.
When tales twist and weave,
We may just believe,
That the fun never rolls out of here.

Verses from a Leafy Glade

In a shaded nook under the sun,
A frog claimed he'd challenge for fun.
With a leap and a splash,
He made quite a crash,
While the muskrats all laughed, one by one.

The daisies wore crowns of fine lace,
As butterflies joined the wild chase.
They spun through the air,
With sparkles to share,
Turning clumsy hops into grace.

A wise owl looked down from his perch,
With a wink, he began a new search.
"Who knows what awaits?
Let's open the gates,
And stroll through the jokes that we birch!"

With humor woven 'twixt branches and roots,
The woodland became full of hoots.
So dance, if you please,
'Neath the giggling trees,
And wear mischief like bright, silly boots.

Songs of the Turning Time

In autumn, the wind sings a tune,
With whispers that playful raccoons croon.
They skitter and dash,
With a giggle and splash,
While leaves swirl like confetti by noon.

A badger, quite stout, joins the fray,
And pretends he could waltz, hip hooray!
But he tripped on a stone,
And rolled like a drone,
Making all of the treetops decay.

"Oh dear!" they'd all shout, "What a sight!"
As the branches all danced with delight.
The critters took part,
With joy in each heart,
For laughter lit up the cool night.

So let every creature partake,
In the laughter that sets our hearts wake.
For when time makes its turn,
And the candles all burn,
We'll cheer for the fun that we make!

Nature's Rhymes Unfurled

In the park, a squirrel pranced,
Eating nuts and doing a dance.
He tripped on a branch,
Oh, what a chance,
As he fell, we all took a glance.

A bird on a limb sang loud,
Chirped a tune that drew a crowd.
It forgot its own song,
And sang all night long,
Leaving us all quite wowed.

A snail with a hat strolled by,
Waving to the clouds so high.
"Good day, Mr. Frog,"
He said with a smog,
"Let's gossip and share a pie!"

The sun set, painting skies of gold,
As shadows grew long and bold.
The critters tucked in,
With a laugh and a grin,
Another good day to behold.

Echoes of the Woodland Tales

In the woods, a wise owl coos,
Telling tales about shoes.
"Don't wear them too tight,
Or you'll take flight,
And lose them to the moose!"

A bunny hopped in with flair,
Wearing sunglasses, such a pair.
With style he did strut,
Feeling quite cut,
He dreamt of hopping in air.

The raccoon held a grand debate,
On whether to scavenge or wait.
With marshmallows stocked,
His plan, well, it rocked,
As he charred them on a plate.

The sun set on woodland's mirth,
Bringing laughter, joy, and worth.
As critters turned in,
With giggles and grins,
They welcomed the dreams of earth.

A Tapestry of Rustling Words

A caterpillar rolled on a leaf,
Claimed it was now a chief.
It summoned its pals,
For fun little jibes,
To share in its newfound belief.

A frog in a top hat appeared,
Said, "None of you must be feared!
Let's leap and let's laugh,
Create a fine draft,
As we dance while the moon is cleared!"

The hedgehog played tunes on a twig,
In a band that was rather big.
With rhythm so bright,
They danced through the night,
While the fireflies lit up the gig.

As dawn broke, the party was grand,
With memories scattered on land.
The critters now snore,
Dreaming of more,
Till the next time they take a stand.

The Ballad of the Changing Season

A chipmunk in winter's coat,
Thought he'd make quite the boat.
He filled it with nuts,
Then sailed with the cuts,
But forgot how to float!

A flurry of snowflakes danced down,
While a skunk wore a tiny crown.
With a puff and a twist,
He made quite a list,
Of critters to wear the town.

The winds brought a chilly surprise,
As squirrels donned scarves in disguise.
"Oh look at us go!"
They shouted, "In snow!
We'll warm up with tales and some pies!"

As spring whispered soft, "Time to play!"
All creatures awoke for the day.
With laughter and cheer,
The change they held dear,
In their hearts, the frost fades away.

Sonnets of the Shifting Boughs

In a grove where the branches do dance,
Squirrels plot their next daring romance.
With acorns as gold,
Their stories unfold,
Jokes whispered in every glance.

A wise owl hoots loudly at night,
As leaves chuckle, a comedic sight.
The moon plays its tune,
While raccoons in a swoon,
Join in on the whimsical flight.

The branches sway low, then they rise,
Tickling the clouds in the skies.
With laughter and cheer,
All creatures draw near,
For comedy's grand surprise.

So gather, all friends, near and far,
Underneath the pale evening star.
Nature's great jest,
At its very best,
In this forest, laughter's the czar.

The Quirks of Season's Change

When autumn dons a vibrant crown,
The pumpkins all wear silly frowns.
With sweaters so bright,
They prance through the night,
In quest of the best leafy gowns.

Spring's breezes cause giggles and glee,
As blossoms dance wild and free.
The bees buzz a tune,
Their antics, a boon,
Creating quite the ruckus, you see.

Summer's heat makes all creatures hop,
With laughter that rises non-stop.
The ice cream's a treat,
As friends laugh and meet,
While the fun never sees a drop.

And winter brings snowman delight,
With scarves that are fuzzy and bright.
Each season's a play,
In a funny ballet,
Where nature is pure, pure delight.

Whimsy Among the Wandering Winds

The breezes tell tales as they twirl,
Of a clumsy old cat on a whirl.
With a jump and a flip,
He takes quite a trip,
While leaves laugh at his dizzying swirl.

In the park, a dog chases air,
With socks on his paws for a flair.
He leaps with pure joy,
Like a playful small boy,
As giggles spring forth everywhere.

There's a dance party under the trees,
Where the branches sway gently with ease.
With frogs in a row,
They steal quite the show,
As crickets provide the melodies.

So let's skip along where it's fun,
Join the laughter till day is done.
In this joyful place,
With humor and grace,
Nature's dance has just begun.

Melodies of the Swaying Treetops

In treetops where melodies fly,
Birds sing with a wink in the sky.
The tunes trickle down,
Change frowns into crowns,
While sunbeams just laugh as they spy.

When gusts play a prank on the pines,
They giggle and bend in straight lines.
With a whoosh and a swoosh,
They laugh in the hush,
Turning moments to playful designs.

Amid the boughs where laughter spills,
The squirrels enact their own thrills.
With flips through the air,
They don't have a care,
As joy dances down through the hills.

So come! Let's sway with the breeze,
Join in on this wild little tease.
For life here's a jest,
Where all are our guests,
In the land of the tickles and trees.

The Magic of Shimmering Shades

In the park, a squirrel in flight,
Chased his tail with all of his might.
A wink from the sun,
Said, "This is real fun!"

A jester on grass, oh so spry,
Told jokes that made passersby cry.
With a tumble and roll,
He stole every soul,

And danced as the clouds drifted by,
Underneath a bright blue, wide sky.
Laughter echoed through trees,
With each wobbly tease.

He vanished at dusk with a leap,
Leaving giggles for all, not a peep.
So remember this hare,
With his whimsical flair.

Serenade of the Golden Hour

As the sun kissed the earth with a grin,
A cheeky little bug danced in spin.
He twirled with delight,
A quirky sight,

His friends tried to mimic the show,
But tripped on the grass like a pro.
With giggles galore,
They fell on the floor,

A raccoon with a hat joined the crew,
"Why not make this a party for two?"
With snacks made of crumbs,
And musical drums,

They sang till the stars fell in view,
A chorus of cha-cha and boo.
So revel in cheer,
When friends gather near!

Whimsy Beneath the Branches

Under branches, a squirrel wore shades,
Sipping juice while he played in the glades.
A breeze brought a cheer,
As friends gathered near,

The shadows began to take form,
As critters played tricks and kept warm.
A dance on the grass,
A wiggle, a pass,

A wise old owl purred in delight,
"Join in, it's a whimsical night!"
With hiccups of fun,
From everyone,

They sang silly songs till the dawn,
With laughter and joy, all were drawn.
So sway with the trees,
And let your heart please!

A Rhyme Among the Tender Twigs

In a garden so lush and so bright,
An ant donned a hat, what a sight!
He rhymed on a whim,
With a skip and a grin,

His friends, they all joined in the play,
As the sun started fading away.
A waltz with some cheer,
Brought giggles so near,

A ladybug twirled on a leaf,
Spinning tales that were utterly brief.
With a wink and a nod,
She danced in the fog,

They laughed till the stars brought their glow,
Pledging friendship, "Let's never say no!"
With a flick and a jump,
The night's just begun!

Sonnet of the Forest Floor

In the woods where giggles grow,
A squirrel dropped his acorn so low.
He danced on a twig,
Doing a jig,
While laughing at the sun's golden glow.

A rabbit hopped by with a grin,
Twirling 'round in a whirl of thin spin.
"Do you hear my new tune?"
Sang a flower in bloom,
As the trees joined the chorus to win.

The mushrooms laid out for a feast,
Inviting all creatures, even the least.
With a wink and a cheer,
They all gathered near,
Sharing stories of mischief and beast.

So here on the floor of the green,
Life tickles the senses, serene.
With a laugh and a play,
It's a comical day,
In a realm where all joy is routine.

Rhythms in the Garden Shade

In the shade where the critters recline,
A hedgehog sipped tea, feeling fine.
He wore a hat snug,
Like a friendly bug,
And hummed an old song that was divine.

The daisies were twisting around,
As butterflies danced with no sound.
"Join in the show!"
Called a sweet doe,
While the breeze played the music profound.

The tomatoes were rolling in style,
Telling jokes with a juicy old smile.
As a cucumber laughed,
And the parsley craft,
They swayed together for quite a while.

So pop by the garden, my friend,
Where the laughter and joy never end.
With a wink from a bee,
Such sweet company,
In the shade, fun and frolic do blend.

Chronicles of the Gentle Breeze

A whispering wind took a stroll,
Playing tag with a cheeky mole.
He chuckled and ran,
With a plan and a can,
To sprinkle some fun from his bowl.

The daisies let out a loud cheer,
As the breeze tickled them, oh so near.
"What mischief you bring!"
Cried the bluebird in spring,
With a song that made laughter appear.

The clouds did a jig in the sky,
As the breeze caught a joke by and by.
"Let's race to the hill!"
Said the thrush with a thrill,
And together they soared, oh my, oh my!

In the valley where colors unite,
The breeze hummed a tune pure delight.
With a chuckle and sigh,
Time drifted on by,
Making memories spark with its flight.

The Poets' Playground in Petals

In a garden of whims, poets play,
With rhymes that hop and sway.
The tulips all pout,
As the poets shout,
"We've found a new game for today!"

The violets giggled in lines,
Crafting jokes with their pretty designs.
"Let's tell a tall tale,
Of a ship with a sail,
And a frog who sipped tea with the pines!"

With a leap and a twirl on green grass,
The daisies joined in with much sass.
"Come join our parade,
Where laughter won't fade,
In this wild, playful world, we amass!"

So when you stroll past this way,
Join the poets who frolic and play.
With a smile and a cheer,
Let yourself steer,
In the joy that the petals display.

Heroes of the Arborous Arc

A squirrel with a cape takes flight,
He battles for acorns each night.
With a flick of his tail,
He'll never go pale,
As he feasts on his spoils of delight.

The raccoon wears a mask with pride,
In the branches, he loves to reside.
He steals shiny things,
On the joy that he brings,
In the forest, he takes quite a stride.

An owl with glasses reads tales,
Of heroes who glide through the gales.
With a hoot and a wink,
He'll pause for a drink,
And let us in on all his trails.

Together they laugh and they play,
In the trees where the critters sway.
With a chirp and a spin,
Let the fun times begin,
In this arboreal cabaret!

The Jive of Deciduous Waltz

Down in the grove under skies,
A group of odd dancers will rise.
With a waddle and jig,
And a leap oh so big,
They twirl till the sunset complies.

The brittle old branches bend low,
To watch as the forest folk glow.
With a twist and a turn,
And some laughter to burn,
They dance 'round the roots in a row.

A chipmunk who taps to the beat,
In his tiny slick shoes, he feels sweet.
With a shuffle and slide,
He'll never deride,
This lively and joyous retreat.

So join in the jive if you dare,
Where the woodland friends frolic and share.
With a bounce and a spin,
Let the fun now begin,
In the waltz of the greenery fair!

Folly Among the Fluttering Shades

A brown bear tried wearing a hat,
But it slipped down to cover his spat.
With berries for lunch,
And a big, silly crunch,
He danced with the shades where he sat.

A hedgehog with pride struts around,
In his armor, he thinks he is crowned.
With a snicker and roll,
He forgets his whole goal,
And tumbles right down to the ground.

The fox with a grin on his snout,
Playfully plans a grand rout.
He'll trick and he'll tease,
With the greatest of ease,
As he sprinkles some chaos throughout.

The forest applauds all the fun,
As their silly antics are spun.
With a giggle and cheer,
They embrace all the weird,
In the folly where laughter is won!

Chronicles Beneath the Canopy

In shadows where whispers arise,
The tall tales take flight through the skies.
With a puff and a puff,
And some giggles quite tough,
The stories bring laughter to ties.

An ant tells a tale of a trip,
Where he rode on a snail with a whip.
With a wiggle and jest,
He claims he is blessed,
Though the snail moves with such a slow slip.

The worm spins a yarn quite absurd,
Of the day that he danced, oh, how stirred!
With a shimmy and shake,
He made critters quake,
And his legend is now widely heard.

Beneath the green canopy's crest,
Where humor and nature are blessed,
The chronicles soar,
And bring joy evermore,
In the heart of the woods, they are pressed!

Lightearted Liveliness in the Grove

In a grove where the giggles grow,
Squirrels dance in a silly show.
A deer trips over a log,
While a rabbit mocks the fog.

The birds chirp tunes that tease,
While the breeze plays with the trees.
A fox, with a wink and a grin,
Challenges a turtle to a spin.

The sun peeks through the green,
Painting shadows, quite a scene.
Each creature shares a laugh,
As they join in the playful staff.

Every branch has a story to tell,
Full of jokes that cast quite a spell.
Where lighthearted spirits soar,
In this grove, there's always more.

The Forest's Humorous Heart

In the heart of the woods so bright,
A hedgehog dances in delight.
He prances with a swagger bold,
While laughing at the stories he's told.

A mouse in a hat thinks he's grand,
Telling tales of a far-off land.
But the truth is, he's just a sage,
Looking for crumbs like a hungry page.

The trees play tricks with shadows long,
While the wind joins in with a song.
Each rustle stirs a jolly rhyme,
Echoing through the halls of time.

With each chuckle, the forest sighs,
Winking at the brightest skies.
Here in this humor-filled space,
Laughter leaves a brilliant trace.

Boughs Beneath a Smiling Sky

Underneath the sky of blue,
The branches wave, a merry crew.
A songbird jests with a twirl,
While a catnapping dog starts to whirl.

The sunbeams flicker like a tease,
Inviting all to dance with ease.
A raccoon dons a mask of cheer,
As a breeze whispers secrets near.

A hedgehog spins like a top,
While fireflies begin to hop.
The moon chuckles at the show,
As stars join in the flow.

With every giggle, shadows dance,
In a playful, bright romance.
So come share in this lively jest,
Beneath the sky, we are blessed.

The Frolic of the Covering Canopy

In the canopy, laughter reigns,
As squirrels play their silly games.
A parrot teaches a crow to sing,
While a spider spins a silky swing.

A raccoon slips on morning dew,
Causing all the birds to coo.
The fox rolls over, free of care,
Barking jokes from up in the air.

The branches jiggle with delight,
As shadows play hide and seek at night.
Beneath this merry overhead,
Every chuckle's just widespread.

In this realm of glee and jest,
Nature's humor is truly blessed.
So heed the cheer, spread the fun,
Join this frolic; it's just begun!

www.ingramcontent.com/pod-product-compliance
Lightning Source LLC
Chambersburg PA
CBHW051630160426
43209CB00004B/587